The season of waiting is here once again. The church, through the liturgy, invites us into a period of active waiting and preparation so that when the Lord comes he will find us with "hearts filled with wonder and praise" (from the Advent II preface). Advent is an invitation to go into the attic of our spiritual home. We are asked to dig through the forgotten treasures of our lives and rediscover the simple joys of our faith.

There is no way we can, or should, turn back the hands of time. Our world is forever moving forward. Progress and change are inevitable. Nevertheless, we are not meant to be passive receptacles of the future. We are to be the creators of our future. We need to carefully examine the changes that enter our lives. We need to discover which elements of the future are gift and should be treasured, and which elements of the future are distortions and should be discarded. In other words, there are old errors and new truths—but there are also old truths and new errors.

Our lives are lived at a hectic pace. Is it too hectic? Our lives are filled to the brim with activities. Is there too much going on in our lives? People were once more honored and respected than they are now. Is there a way to rediscover that people are more important than things? Yes; but this will never happen unless we are willing to change.

*With Hearts Full of Wonder* is written to help us make whatever changes are necessary in our lives right now. Each day of this booklet starts with a brief passage from one of the lectionary readings which will help us to focus on a particular aspect of Advent waiting. Next there is a reflection on the Scripture that will enable us to connect Jesus' words with our own lives. This is followed by a brief prayer that echoes the reflection. Finally, a meditation is offered to help us evaluate and initiate whatever changes we may need to make in order to become better Christians this Advent.

Advent awaits our attention. If we can step outside the habitual and rediscover lost religious truths, then Advent can be a time of active waiting that changes our lives and our world. In this spirit, my dear brothers and sisters, let us together actively wait for the birth of our Savior.

# First Sunday of Advent

*You know the time in which we are living. It is now the hour for you to wake from sleep, for our salvation is closer than when we first accepted the faith.* ROM 13:11–14

Hardly anyone likes to get out of bed in the morning. When the alarm rings we hit the snooze button and roll over for a few more minutes, wrapped in the seductive arms of sleep. Our lives can be like that, too. Most of the time we are sleepwalking Christians; at worst we are sound asleep, our Christian deeds but a dream. Advent is our wake-up call. The challenge is to hear the call and not roll over and fall back into our Christian lethargy. It is time to cast off the darkness, to clear out the junk that clutters our lives.

Here is a powerful story that will set the tone for Advent. As Eddie and his father are saying their evening prayers, his father leans over and pats Eddie on the chest, just below his heart and says, "Do you know what is in there?" Eddie looks at his father and says, "Guts!" They both laugh, then his father says, "And what else?" Eddie looks at his father and says, "I don't know." The father smiles, saying, "A piece of God!" Then his father pats himself and says, "What's in here?" Eddie smiles: "Guts…and a piece of God!" The game continues. "What's in mom, Aunt Nancy and Uncle Louie, your sister Sally?" Eddie shouts out, "A piece of God." Finally Eddie's father asks him what is in Alberta, the spoiled brat in Eddie's second-grade class. Eddie hesitates, saying "Guts"; his father insists, "And what else?" Eddie looks at his father and tells him that no, all Alberta has in her is guts. His father patiently explains that everyone has a piece of God. Eddie, with the wisdom given to the young, grudgingly accepts that Alberta has a piece of God, but adds: "Her piece must be covered with a bunch of junk!"

Advent is all about rediscovering the piece of God within us and removing the junk that prevents us from letting the piece of God shine out in our lives and on our world.

## Prayer:

*Lord, when I am tempted to remain asleep in my darkness, rouse me to give witness to your light.*

## Meditation:

What is the junk that is covering up my piece of God?

# Monday of the First Week

*As Jesus entered Capernaum, a centurion approached him with this request: "Sir, my serving boy is at home in bed paralyzed, suffering painfully." He said to him, "I will come and cure him." "Sir," the centurion said in reply, "I am not worthy to have you under my roof. Just give an order and my boy will get better."*

MT 8:5–11

Today's gospel tells us about the strong faith of the centurion, who believed that Jesus had only to say a word for the boy to be cured. It reminds us that there is a fine line between faith and superstition, between miracles and magic. Do these examples sound familiar? Our daughter is getting married and the forecast calls for rain, so we hang rosary beads out the window. We are selling our house, so we bury a statue of St. Joseph upside down in the front lawn. We are going in for a swim and dip our right hand into the water to make a sign of the cross. Are these gestures faith in action or superstition? Only in our hearts do we know for certain.

Just before communion, at every celebration of the Eucharist, we pray as the centurion did: "Lord, I am not worthy to receive you, but only say the word and my soul will be healed." Of course we are unworthy of God. Fortunately, God loves us whether we are worthy or not. Better still, God's love makes us worthy: that is the whole point of God, the whole point of love. Love is a gift freely given; it cannot be earned. Did we earn our parents' love? Of course not: parents love us regardless of who we are. Do we earn a friend's love? No. Friendship is love freely given.

One of the biggest challenges of faith is to receive God's love without trying to earn that love. We feel better when we think we can earn love, because by so doing we are able to be in charge. But God loves us despite anything we do or say; our only response can be to say "thank you" with the lives we live.

**Prayer:**

*Lord, where would I be without the love you so freely give to me? I will show my gratitude by being true to your word.*

**Meditation:**

What superstition needs to be weeded out of my faith practices?

# Tuesday of the First Week

*Turning to his disciples he said to them privately: "Blest are the eyes that see what you see. I tell you, many prophets and kings wished to see what you see but did not see it, and to hear what you hear but did not hear it."* LK 10:21– 24

In order to see things clearly we need to have either a good guide or proper training. A dentist can take a look in our mouths and know that we grind our teeth at night. A mechanic takes one look at the tires and knows that our car is out of alignment. An antiques dealer can look at a piece of jewelry and know what it is worth.

Some people looked at Jesus and saw a carpenter; others saw a messiah. All too often we see what we want to see, rather than what is really there. This became clear to me when I was once the victim of a surprise birthday party. Looking back after the party, there were many clues that something was up: people who were not where they normally would have been, phone calls that were obviously bogus. Nevertheless, I saw what I wanted to see and was led to be surprised.

Many years ago, in one of my first assignments, I was bilked out of some money by a clever con team. A well-dressed gentleman rang the rectory doorbell one evening. He told me his wife was having an affair. He had followed her and caught her with the other man. While he was playing amateur detective, someone had slashed two of the tires on his car. Now he had a problem. He had to be at work at a local trucking company by nine o'clock that evening or he would lose his job. He gave me the name of the company and a telephone number so that I could verify his story. Sure enough, his boss answered the phone, thanked me for helping out, and asked me to call a taxi and pay the driver. The company would send me a check in the morning to cover the cost. When the check failed to arrive, I eventually realized I had been taken in by a clever story.

## Prayer:

*Lord, open my eyes and my ears that I may come to know the life you want me to live.*

## Meditation:

Where are the signs of God's presence in my life and why do I miss them so easily?

# Wednesday of the First Week

*He took the seven loaves and the fish, and after giving thanks he broke them and gave them to the disciples, who in turn gave them to the crowd. All ate until they were full.* MT 15:29–37

One of the most persistent challenges in life is to give new meaning to well-known stories. The same is true of our faith. Over the years my understanding of the multiplication of the loaves and fish has changed. Like most people, I always assumed that the new bread and fish were created on the spot, pulled from nothingness by God through the intervention of Jesus. In some ways, this miracle seemed like a divine magic show.

Could it be the miracle which occurred was that human hearts were changed, that generosity was multiplied? Today's gospel tells us the people with Jesus for three days had had nothing to eat. Perhaps this means that the crowd never ate as a group. People may have eaten on the sly because they were afraid that there might not be enough food to go around. They did not want to share with the others who had just run off to follow Jesus and had not thought to bring food.

Jesus got the crowd to sit down, think about food, thank God for the food they had, bless the food, and share. It was the sharing that became infectious. Because Jesus did not hoard what he and the disciples had, others decided not to hoard what they had. In so doing they discovered two very important things: they had more than they needed and they did not need as much as they thought.

Advent is a great time to think about what we have, what we need, and how we can share more generously. The examination of conscience from Leonard Bernstein's *Mass* can guide us in discovering how to be more caring in our sharing: "What I need I don't have, what I have I don't own, what I own I don't want, what I want, Lord, I don't know…."

**Prayer:**

*Lord, by your example I see that all people are my sisters and brothers. Teach me your generous ways.*

**Meditation:**

What do I really want from life? What must I do to find this?

# Thursday of the First Week

*Jesus said to his disciples: "None of those who cry out, 'Lord, Lord,' will enter the kingdom of God but only the one who does the will of my Father in heaven." MT 7:21, 24–27*

Would that we could be saved just by our words and our prayers. But God is on to us. God knows that we hide too easily behind words, get carried away with them and say more than we mean. The easy way out would be to say, "It is human nature to say one thing and do another," but that is about as convincing as "Everyone is doing it." God does not want our excuses; God wants our life.

The difference between our words and our deeds was brought home to me in a powerful way a number of years ago. One of the most challenging aspects of pastoral ministry is helping people cope with death. Without being totally aware of it, I had developed the habit of saying to grieving families, "If there is anything I can do, just ask." I do not know how many times I had said that phrase without ever being asked to do anything. But one day I said it to a family reeling from a violent and tragic death. The next thing I knew I was in the morgue identifying the body for the family. I still say to people, "If there is anything I can do, just ask," but I no longer say it thoughtlessly. I say it knowing full well that it can end up leading somewhere I normally would not choose to go.

Advent calls us to reflect on what we say and how we live. When we say "I love you," do we sometimes really mean, "I like you"? Do we say "I believe in God…" when what we really mean is "I believe…provided God does not intrude in my life too much"? We know the feeling of betrayal when a friend says, "I give you my word…" but does not honor that word. What does it mean to God when we pray and make professions of faith, yet do not live lives worthy of our calling?

**Prayer:**

*Lord, you give us the power of speech, but so often we abuse this with empty words. Help me to mean what I say.*

**Meditation:**

How can I grow into the prayers and promises which I make to God?

# Friday of the First Week

*As Jesus moved on from Capernaum, two blind men came after him crying out, "Son of David, have pity on us!" When he got to the house, the blind men caught up with him.* MT 9:27–31

Well, what do you know: we are like Jesus after all—at least the Jesus in today's gospel! The gospel clearly says "the blind men caught up with him," which implies that Jesus heard the blind men call out for help and kept right on walking. We may not think about it too often, but the human Jesus had to grow into being the Messiah. In much the same way we have to continue to grow into being the daughters and sons of God.

One thing is certain: there will always be someone crying out for help. This has forced many of us who are better off to develop a defense mechanism that enables us not to see, hear, or pay attention to certain individuals. We can see starving people on TV and not be moved to action; we can read of those who live below the poverty level and not think of how obscene it is for anyone to live in poverty in a land of plenty. Often, those who are in need are closer to home: a daughter or son wants help with homework, yet we stay immersed in our own work. A wife is waiting for an affirming word, a husband, to be thanked. A neighbor hopes for a visit, a parent craves a "Hi-I-was-just-thinking-about-you" call.

When the blind men caught up with Jesus, he restored their sight and made them whole. What needs to change in our life and with our priorities so that those who hurry behind us, looking for help, can catch up with us? What must we do so that these people can become whole? Just as Jesus could not become the Messiah until he heard the cries of those who surrounded him, so too we will not be fully whole and Christian until we hear—and answer—the cries of those in need.

## Prayer:

*Lord, so often I take what I have for granted, and shut out the needs of those around me. As I wait to celebrate your birth at Christmas, let me be more compassionate to the cries of others.*

## Meditation:

What group, agency, or individual has been calling out to me? Do I hear that call as the call of God to live my faith more fully?

# Saturday of the First Week

*No longer will your Teacher hide himself, but with your own eyes you shall see your Teacher, while from behind, a voice shall sound in your ears: "this is the way; walk in it," when you would turn to the right or to the left.* IS 30:19–21, 23–26

One of the attributes of modern living which I personally find annoying is the Occupational Safety and Health Administration requirement that all trucks, buses, and heavy equipment must be equipped with an alarm which sounds whenever the vehicle backs up. The practical me knows that lives are saved by these alarms; the romantic me wonders why we need more noise pollution in a world afraid of silence.

In today's first reading Isaiah reminds us that God, our teacher, is always showing us where to walk and how to live. The problem is that we try to ignore the voice of God. Perhaps God could borrow the alarm concept from OSHA. What would happen if God were to fit us with an alarm that would sound a warning every time we began to wander from the straight and narrow? Imagine we are reaching for the bottle to pour that one last drink which we really do not need: "blaaah" goes the alarm. We are stopped by a policeman and are about to lie and say we did not realize we were going so fast: "blaaah" goes the alarm. We are taking an important test and our eyes begin to wander to our neighbor's paper in search of an answer; we call in sick and the boss cannot hear us because of the alarm going off.

It is a good thing we are not fitted with such alarms, because the world would be filled with unbearable noise. The fact is that God loves us too much to try to embarrass us into doing the right thing. God whispers in our ear, gently guiding us along right paths. When we wander God urges us to return. We don't need an alarm that announces our transgressions. What we really need is to realize we are loved and follow the voice of God, freely walking in God's ways.

## Prayer:

*Lord, you watch over me with care and concern. Guide my feet along the straight and narrow pathway.*

## Meditation:

Can I take the time today to be still enough to hear the whisper of God's voice in my ear?

# Second Sunday of Advent

*John was clothed in a garment of camel's hair and wore a leather belt around his waist. Grasshoppers and wild honey were his food. At that time Jerusalem, all Judea, and the whole region around the Jordan were going out to him.* MT 3:1–12

Somehow I cannot picture myself going out into the desert to see a weirdo dressed funny and eating all kinds of strange things. I have all I can do to stay focused while talking to a young man with several earrings or an orange-haired women with nose studs. I am ashamed to admit that I let unimportant "things" get in the way.

Some years ago I read a story about the rector of a cathedral in a major city, who asked a friend of his to be the guest homilist at an important celebration. The rector's priest friend agreed to preach but told the rector not to be alarmed if he were not there for the beginning of the celebration. The appointed day came. The rector looked for his friend, but started the celebration without him. At the gospel, the rector began to proclaim the words about giving places of honor to the wealthy and well-dressed while discriminating against those who are poor and wear ill-fitting clothes. As he was reading, a homeless person entered the cathedral. He was unshaven, a bit ripe in his fragrance, and smelled of cheap wine. The bum stopped every three or four rows and tried to get people to make room for him. The entire congregation ignored him. Not finding a welcome in the congregation, the bum entered the sanctuary and got to the pulpit just as the rector was holding up the gospels, saying, "The good news of the Lord." He pushed the rector out of the way as two ushers quickly sprang to the pastor's defense. The pastor waved them off as he recognized the bum as his friend, the guest preacher. The bum/preacher then began his homily: "How could you listen to this gospel and feel no inclination to live what you have just heard?"

Advent is a time to identify and root out the prejudices that blind us to the presence of God in all people.

## Prayer:

*Lord, touch my heart; may I truly live your gospel message.*

## Meditation:

What are the "things" which get in the way so that I cannot see the beauty and truth in the world?

# Monday of the Second Week

*Some men came along carrying a paralytic on a mat. They were trying to bring him in and lay him before Jesus; but they found no way of getting him through because of the crowd, so they went up on the roof. There they let him down with his mat through the tiles into the middle of the crowd before Jesus.* LK 5:17–26

On a college retreat some years ago, I invited the students to take today's gospel, to read it prayerfully, and then see with whom they identified. The answers were powerful, and I experienced parts of today's gospel that I had never even considered.

One student identified with the man who went out of his way to loan Jesus the use of his house. He knew it would be an honor for him to have this well-known, itinerant preacher in his home; perhaps Jesus would work a miracle there. In the end, we never learn his name and he ends up with a hole in his roof. I wonder if he stayed a believer once he realized what his faith in Jesus was going to cost? Other students identified with the friends who carried the paralytic. They talked about the ways their best intentions sometimes did not work out. They related that they could be late in offering assistance, or were sometimes insensitive to the needs of the people they were trying to help.

Still others identified with those who arrived on time, got a seat up close to Jesus, then were displaced by the people who arrived late and removed the roof tiles. They talked about getting easily aggravated by people who act in irresponsible ways. They talked about the need to be aware that the pain of others sometimes pushes them to act in bold and dramatic ways.

Not one student identified with Jesus or with the paralytic. Yet as Christians, we, like the paralytic when he was cured, are called to continue the work of Jesus. As sinners we need to receive forgiveness and healing from our God, each and every day.

### Prayer:

*Lord, when I am tempted to overlook the forgiveness and healing which you offer, let me reach out to you instead.*

### Meditation:

If I were to see myself as Jesus alive in our world, what would change most in my life?

---

# Tuesday of the Second Week

*Jesus said to his disciples, "What is your thought on this: A man owns a hundred sheep and one of them wanders away; will he not leave the ninety-nine out on the hills and go in search of the stray?"* MT 18:12–14

In today's gospel one sheep wanders and ninety-nine stay put. In our day, it seems that ninety-nine wander and one stays put. This is especially true during Advent. How many of us are truly trying to make the most of the religious aspect of preparation? How many have just given up, caved in, and followed the crowd? A voice still cries out in the desert, "Make ready the way of the Lord"; yet fewer and fewer ears are attuned to hear that voice. It was a very wise and holy person who first observed that God visits us frequently; the problem is that we are most often not home.

The image of the Good Shepherd reflects the patient, forgiving love of God; the emphasis is not on how many of us need that patient, forgiving love. We all wander from the path of goodness and from the path of justice. We are unfaithful to our God and to each other. But our wandering is not the focus of this gospel: God's searching is.

In a very real sense, God is out to get us. He will track us down. Francis Thompson, in his poem *The Hound of Heaven*, beautifully describes our attempts to escape the God who is following us: "I fled Him down the nights and down the days;/ I fled Him down the arches of the years;/ I fled Him down the labyrinthine ways of my own mind;/ and in the mist of tears I hid from Him…." Rather than focus on our wandering, we need to focus on God's luxuriant and irrepressible love. If we show the least interest in returning to God, in coming home and getting back on the straight path, God will be there to meet us.

**Prayer:**

*Lord, when I wander you look for me; when I fall you gather me in your arms. Thank you for your watchfulness.*

**Meditation:**

Where have I wandered from the true spirit of Advent? What needs to happen if I am to allow God to get me back on track?

# Wednesday of the Second Week

*Come to me, all you who are weary and find life burdensome, and
I will refresh you. Take my yoke upon your shoulders and learn
from me, for I am gentle and humble of heart.* MT 11:28–30

Jesus says, "Come to me…." Most of us would like him to say, "I
will come to you and make everything better. Don't worry, I will
take care of you." God watches us from the inside out and the outside in. The Almighty knows all about our moods, wants, and needs but
loves us enough to lie back and wait for us to take some initiative with our
lives. Our God is a loving and forgiving God, not a rescuing God. God lives
the wisdom behind this lovely aphorism, "Give a person a fish and she will
eat for a day; teach that same person how to fish and she will eat for a lifetime!"

In order to be refreshed and to have our burdens eased, we must hear the
invitation to draw near to God and admit our need. Most of us have been
taught to feel ashamed of being in need. We love to help our friends in their
time of need but we are not as open to receiving help from our friends. When
someone tells us that they were stretched to the limit just last week, we listen. We get furious when we learn a friend was in need and did not reach out
to us; would that we get as furious with ourselves when we are too embarrassed to ask for help. Asking for help is very difficult.

The journey back to God is likewise difficult. We want to go to God with
everything in order; we do not want to appear needy, even to God. We want
all the world to come to our doorstep with their problems so we can feel
good about helping. When it is our turn to be in need, however, we run away
and hide. We love to give help and are loath to ask for help. This is another
human contradiction for us to consider on our Advent journey.

### Prayer:

*Lord, teach me to be open to receiving help from you and from my neigh-
bor when I am in need.*

### Meditation:

Henri Nouwen observed, "If I can only give and not receive, the only honest thing to do is to question why I give." Where do I need to be more open
to receive God's love and less preoccupied with trying to earn that love?

# Thursday of the Second Week

*From John the Baptizer's time until now the kingdom of God has suffered violence, and the violent take it by force.* MT 11:11–15

The kingdom of God has certainly suffered violence. There is no doubt, too, that our world is all too often a place of violence and force. Look at all the people who live in fear. One of my favorite cartoons from the *New Yorker* magazine expresses very well the tension between the kingdom of God and the violence of our world: a man is inside his apartment, exhausted, leaning up against a front door that is laden with every conceivable kind of lock and security device, while under the door someone has slipped a valentine card.

Signs of violence are part of everyday life. Schools have locked doors and metal detectors. We barricade ourselves in our homes, carry mace in our purses, take self-defense courses, and carry guns for protection. We would not think of owning a car without an alarm system. I was recently in the parking lot of my parish one Sunday, and was overwhelmed by the symphony of car alarms beeping as the owners approached to enter their cars. To me, this sound was even more depressing than the parking lot driving habits of many of the "redeemed," who push in front of their fellow parishioners just to get out of the lot a few minutes earlier—having just shared both Eucharist and a sign of peace with these same neighbors. It often seems as if the violence of the world is setting the agenda for our lives.

One classic confrontation between violence and the kingdom of God is the issue of capital punishment. Too many Christians believe that using violence to curb violence will solve the problem. Too many of us who are in favor of capital punishment fail to appreciate that the spirit of punishment and revenge which we cling to in our righteousness does violence to the kingdom of God.

### Prayer:

*O Lord, you are the God of peacefulness and compassion. Help me to know your ways and walk in love for my neighbor.*

### Meditation:

How do I add to the violence that threatens to overrun the world?

# Friday of the Second Week

*Yet time will prove where wisdom lies.* MT 11:16–19

Advent is all about waiting, all about time. It is about celebrating the gift of time and being thankful that we get second chances, that we have the opportunity to grow and to change and to develop our gifts and talents.

I recently unearthed a copy of a college newspaper which contained an article of mine. At first, I was embarrassed; the article was not well-written. I had the same feeling that I get when I look at an old photograph of myself. I know that the picture is me but I do not like what I see and hope that no one I know ever sees the photo. Believe me, I didn't want anyone I know to see my college article! Then I began to think: if I wrote the article today, it would definitely be an embarrassment. When I wrote the article, however, it was no doubt as good as I could have written then.

We are very lucky people because we are never limited to what we have done or achieved in life thus far. Our past accomplishments are but a staircase to future growth and improvement. There is a story that brings out this message. A tourist was passing through a sleepy southern town. Eager to find out what famous people might have been born in the town he went up to an old gentleman who was peacefully rocking on his front porch. The tourist asked, "Any famous people born here?" The old gentleman kept rocking and said, "Nope, just babies."

No one is born famous. We have to work, develop our skills, make mistakes, make progress, get discouraged, be energized. Most of all we have to stick with it. We are all familiar with the adage, "If something is worth doing, it is worth doing well"; there is truth in that bit of wisdom. The truth is, we can learn not only from our mistakes but from our fledgling attempts to master a new behavior or skill. Advent teaches us that we have the time to wait, to show patience in becoming who God intended us to be.

## Prayer:

*Lord, through the grace of this season, let me reflect on the gifts you have given me and remember to use them for your glory.*

## Meditation:

In what area of my life have I given up? Where have I stopped trying to grow and improve?

# Saturday of the Second Week

*To turn back the hearts of fathers toward their sons and to reestablish the tribes of Jacob. Blessed is he who shall have seen you before he dies.* SIR 48:1–4, 9–11

What a great theme for Advent: fathers and mothers turned back toward their children. Advent should be proclaimed as a family time, a time of hearts speaking to hearts, wounds healed, hands reaching out to bridge the gaps that inevitably spring up in our relationships. What better way to prepare for the birth of our Savior than to turn back to our mothers and fathers, brothers and sisters, husbands and wives, sons and daughters, and reestablish the ties that often become frayed with the passage of time?

Several years ago, I ran into a man I knew from a previous parish. We were both out shopping for Christmas presents, both in a hurry. In the course of our brief conversation I found out that he had recently gone through an unpleasant divorce, and that he and his former wife were still angry at each other. Now he was out Christmas shopping for the first time in years. He told me the only thing that made the shopping tolerable was that he knew he was going to be able to spend more money on gifts for his children than his ex-wife could, and that buying the children's attention while alienating his former wife was going to be very satisfying.

My face gave away my reaction, and the man asked what was wrong. I quickly rattled off my observations: I thought using Christmas presents as a wedge between children and a parent was obscene, and that spending money in anger to punish someone was not in the spirit of Christmas. I told him I thought he should call his former wife, find a way to share the cost of presents, and not have gifts from mom and gifts from dad. He then said that he was sorry he had asked me what was wrong; I told him I was, too, and we shared an awkward good-bye. I do not know what he did after that, but I pray he was able to turn the hearts of a father and mother, who were no longer husband and wife, back to their children.

## Prayer:

*Lord, melt my hardened heart; help me to turn back.*

## Meditation:

Before Christmas, will I have the courage to mend at least one broken relationship?

# Third Sunday of Advent

*John in prison heard about the works Christ performed, and sent a message through his disciples to ask him, "Are you 'He who is to come' or do we look for another?"* MT 11:2–11

It is John the Baptizer—the one who was sent into the world to point the way to the messiah, the one who did not want to baptize Jesus because he was unworthy, the one who pointed to Jesus in the crowd and said, "Behold the Lamb of God"—who is filled with questions. Today's gospel carries the important message that it is all right to question and doubt. Somewhere along the line asking questions and raising doubt have developed a bad reputation with organized religion. This should not be, because doubt leads to questions, questions lead to answers, and answers lead to growth. In today's gospel, John is honest enough to share his questions and doubts with his disciples. He then delivers his questions to Jesus. Because he shared his doubts, Jesus was able to answer John, and he and his disciples were strengthened in their faith.

One of the more enjoyable aspects of being a parish priest is when people ask sincere questions about their faith, deep and profound questions that are shared like precious gems: "Can I feel the way I do about certain issues and still be a Catholic?" "I know the church is opposed to divorce but I am not sure how to reconcile that teaching with the reality of my situation." "What happens if I cannot find a way to forgive my brother?" "Do you think God really hears my prayers?" "How can I believe in a good God when there is so much evil in the world?"

I will bet you have at least one repressed question lying just beneath the surface of your faith. Why not follow the example of John the Baptist and share that question with a friend or with your parish priest? As someone once said, "Live the question and, without knowing how, you will live into the answer." Now that is faith!

## Prayer:

*Lord, you know my heart; you see my questions and doubts. Despite these, I truly believe in your everlasting love and mercy; I believe that you are the God of all.*

## Meditation:

What question needs to see the light of day during this time of preparation for the birth of our Savior?

# Monday of the Third Week

*Jesus answered: "I too will ask a question. If you answer it for me, then I will tell you on what authority I do the things I do. What was the origin of John's baptism? Was it divine or merely human?" Their answer to Jesus was, "We do not know."* MT 21:23–27

There is a scene in the movie *Ordinary People* that has given me one of my favorite quotes. In the movie, Judd Hirsch plays a psychiatrist who is trying to help a young man recover from the guilt he feels because his brother drowned in a freak storm, while he survived. Every time the boy is asked a difficult question he answers, "I do not know." The psychiatrist is gentle with the boy. At first, he lets the "I do not know" answer go unquestioned. But as the healing relationship intensifies he must challenge what is really a technique of denial. Finally, Hirsch's character says to the boy, "Why don't you leave the 'I don't knows' out on the table with the magazines?" (People who have come to me for pastoral counseling over the years will smile when they read this because they have often heard this line from me in our time together!)

Sometimes, when we really do not know the answer, we make up an answer. But when we *do* know the answer and are ashamed, embarrassed, or afraid to say it out loud, we say, "I don't know." We hide from reality by feigning ignorance. Here are a few examples: when we are asked why we still resent a person for an offense long since grown old, it sounds so much better to say, "I don't know" than to say "Because I am a spiteful person who wants the satisfaction of revenge." When someone asks why we are not more generous in sharing our possessions or give less than we can afford to a worthy cause, "I don't know" is much softer than saying "Because I am an insecure person who clings to my things in the fear that without them I am nothing."

A true "I don't know" requires great humility. A bogus "I don't know" leads only to stagnation.

## Prayer:

*Lord, give me the eyes to honestly look at myself.*

## Meditation:

Where in my life do I claim ignorance as an excuse to not change what should be changed in the way I am living?

# Tuesday of the Third Week

*There was a man who had two sons. He approached the elder and said, "Son, go out and work in the vineyard today." The son replied, "I am on my way, sir;" but he never went. Then the man came to the second son and said the same thing. This son said in reply, "No, I will not;" but afterward he regretted it and went.* MT 21:28–32

When I was a little boy, I frequently put more food on my plate than I could eat. When I put it on my plate, I was sure I could eat it all, but it seemed I always overestimated my capacity. On such occasions my mother would always recite a little poem, "Remember the pelican,/ its bill can hold more than its belly can!"

When it comes to being a Christian, our mouths are frequently bigger than our deeds: we are all guilty of talking a good game. At the beginning of Advent, most of us promised that this year was going to be different. We were not going to get caught up in the pre-Christmas hype; we were going to remember the true purpose of Advent. This was going to be the year when some sanity would return to our preparation for the birth of our Savior. Unfortunately, our deeds of faith are too much like a well-intentioned diet: lost in a tomorrow that never comes.

Today's gospel gives us two extremes. In doing so it obscures, at least for the moment, that the best response to the invitation to work in God's vineyards is to say "yes!" and then do it. The parable which Jesus tells today is intended primarily to give us hope. It calls us to examine our lives and ask: are we doing what God wants us to do? If the answer is "no," then there is no time like the present to start shaping our lives according to gospel values. If the answer to that question is "yes," then there is no better time to thank God for the freedom to choose the will of God, and to look for new and better ways to be good Christian men and women.

## Prayer:

*Lord, sometimes my words seem full of empty promises. Today, let me thank you for the times when I have been able to keep my promises to you and to others.*

## Meditation:

How true have I been to my promise to honor the season of Advent? What needs to change now?

# Wednesday of the Third Week

*Jesus gave this response: "Go and report to John what you have seen and heard. The blind recover their sight, cripples walk, lepers are cured, the deaf hear, dead persons are raised to life, and the poor have the good news preached to them."* LK 7:18–23

Today's gospel highlights the fact that it is much easier to say the right thing than to do what is right. Many years ago, on a dreary Belgian morning, I was walking with a group of fellow students to theology class at the University of Louvain. Up ahead of us, coming our way, was a young priest dressed in a black cassock. Head cast down, left hand grasping an overstuffed and battered leather briefcase, his entire mien was dark and unwelcoming.

As he drew almost even with our group, we offered a greeting in American-accented French. He never paused, never hesitated, never lifted his eyes in recognition, nor even took the time to grunt a return greeting. He purposefully stormed on toward his destination. The young priest was almost past us when from the back of our group a voice solemnly said, "He would have said hello but he was late for the defense of his doctoral dissertation, 'Christ in the Human Encounter.'" It was a moment of laughter, as well as a very important lesson: it is one thing to know the gospel but quite another thing to live it!

When Jesus was asked if he was the messiah, he did not answer "yes" or "no." Jesus answered with his life. He pointed out how he had fulfilled all the biblical signs of the messiah: the blind see, the lame walk, and the poor have the good news preached to them. When someone asks us if we are Christian, are we at least a bit embarrassed that our Christianity is so well hidden that the question had to be asked in the first place? When it comes to our faith, it should be worn on our sleeve. Advent is the time to make sure our hearts are in the right place.

## Prayer:

*Lord, you bring miracles into the lives of those who believe. Let me always put my faith and trust in you.*

## Meditation:

Where do I see Christ in my everyday life? Am I passing up the opportunity to encounter him more and more?

---

# Thursday of the Third Week

*O Wisdom, O holy Word of God, you govern all creation with your
strong yet tender care. Come and show your people
the way to salvation.*
—EVENING PRAYER FROM THE LITURGY OF THE HOURS

We like to think that we alone can bring about our salvation. The truth is that God does the work if we only listen and pay attention. God's wisdom is expressed in many ways but primarily through the Hebrew and Christian Scriptures. As the pace of Christmas becomes more and more hectic, the Word of God will be pushed more and more into the background. God's wisdom will be shunned for the wisdom of the world. But God will remain strong, yet tender: strong in love for us, tender in patient waiting for us to turn back to divine wisdom.

Strong, yet tender is a beautiful description of God; it is also a beautiful description of parents. Advent is a natural time to be appreciative of our parents. If they are still alive, we can plan to pay them a visit or give them a call. We can tell them that we love them, and how much we appreciate all that they do and have done for us. If we are not fortunate enough to have our parents still with us, we can visit them in our minds. We can dredge up some of the horror stories of our past, and remember some of the good times we shared in the home. Our mental visit with our parents can end with a prayer of thanksgiving for their patient understanding and tender care.

If our family life was difficult, and our parents less than loving, we can take some time to reflect on the ways they may have tried to show care and concern for us. This may be a good time to let go of past hurts and ask God to help us reconcile the wrongs of our childhood. Perhaps this is the year we celebrate the birth of Jesus in our hearts by leaving behind the hurt that has kept us from truly knowing the joy of Christmas.

## Prayer:

*Lord, fill me with tenderness and strength that I may reflect your love to all.*

## Meditation:

What are some of the pleasant memories of my parents' love?

# Friday of the Third Week

*O sacred Lord of ancient Israel, who showed yourself to Moses in*
*the burning bush, who gave him the holy law on Sinai mountain:*
*come, stretch out your hand and set us free.*
—EVENING PRAYER FROM THE LITURGY OF THE HOURS

Today we are reminded of the power of God manifested in salvation history. The prayer of the Church reminds us that we have been given a holy law by God; this law is written in our hearts. God rescued the chosen people from captivity in Egypt and set them on the road of Exodus. The Jews, our ancestors in faith, wandered for forty years before they arrived at the promised land. During that journey they more than once expressed frustration with God. They cried out in hunger: God gave them manna. The people moaned, grumbled, and complained: God listened patiently. The chosen people got water from a rock to satisfy their thirst and a pillar of fire to guide their journey. God's desire to set the faithful free is never exhausted.

Sir Francis Drake has a great prayer that can enrich our final days of Advent. "Disturb us, Lord, when we are too well pleased with ourselves; when our dreams have come true because we have dreamed too little; when we have arrived safely because we sailed too close to shore. Disturb us, Lord, when with the abundance of things we possess we have lost our thirst for the abundance of life; having fallen in love with life, we have ceased to dream of eternity. And in the efforts to build a new earth, we have allowed our vision of the new heaven to dim. Disturb us, Lord, to dare more boldly, to venture on wider seas where storms will show your mastery; where losing sight of the land, we shall find the stars. We ask you to push back the horizons of our hopes; and to push us toward the future in strength, courage, faith, hope, and love."

Soon, very soon, we will be asked to follow the light of a star. Are we ready to heed the call?

**Prayer:**

*Lord, stretch out your hand and set me free from that which enslaves me.*

**Meditation:**

Where am I too pleased with myself? Can I freely ask God to disturb that aspect of my life?

# Saturday of the Third Week

*O Flower of Jesse's stem, you have been raised up as a sign for all peoples; kings stand silent in your presence; the nations bow down in worship before you. Come, let nothing keep you from coming to our aid.* —EVENING PRAYER FROM THE LITURGY OF THE HOURS

We are a people who ignore signs. We run stop signs; we park in "no parking" zones; we are immune to warnings on the side of cigarette packages. Most of us pay no attention to freshness dates on food containers. A wet paint sign almost forces us to touch the paint to make sure the sign is correct. And yet God comes to us as sign.

Whenever I think of signs, I think of my father, who taught my three brothers and me how to drive. My father is a mostly patient, laconic, almost taciturn man. Older brother would pass on to next-in-line brother a phrase my father was certain to use while teaching us to drive: "The sign says *stop*, not *wait*." My father was basically a law and order man, but stop signs brought out his only liberal tendency. He would stop but he would not wait unless absolutely necessary, and he taught his sons to do likewise. In the case of stop signs my father taught a very important lesson: do what the sign says but then move on; don't get stuck.

When it comes to the signs of God, we have to do the same. God is present in the beauty of a sunset or sunrise; is God present in the rain? God is present in the joy of new birth; is God present in the emptiness of death? God is present in our togetherness; is God present in our solitude? Wherever the sign of God's presence speaks to us is a treasured experience but it is not the end of God's presence. It is one sign among many. The trick is not to get stuck. We need to remain open to new experiences of God.

As Christmas approaches and we find God's presence in the manger, the music, the cards, and the presents, can we also find God in our preparation, in our quiet, in the bits and pieces of reflective time we hollow out during the last few days of Advent?

## Prayer:

*Lord, come to my aid! I am listening for your footsteps.*

## Meditation:

What new signs—if any—of God's presence have I discovered during this Advent season?

# Fourth Sunday of Advent

*When his mother Mary was engaged to Joseph, but before they lived together, she was found with child through the power of the Holy Spirit. Joseph her husband, an upright man unwilling to expose her to the law, decided to divorce her quietly.* MT 1:18–24

The story of the birth of Jesus is so familiar that we sometimes miss the tension in the account. We imagine that Mary and Joseph knew how everything was going to work out, and fail to understand the depth of their faith.

Today's gospel says that Joseph was going to divorce Mary quietly. How do you think *that* was going to happen? Everyone in their small town knew they were engaged. If Joseph broke off the engagement and then Mary had a baby, everyone would know that Joseph was not the father; everyone would wonder who the father was and Mary's reputation would be ruined. This "special" pregnancy had the potential to ruin the lives of two very good people. Only faith—strong, personal faith—was able to save the day.

Mary had to find a way to say "yes" to God; Joseph had to find a way to join that "yes" and make it his own. Neither Mary nor Joseph knew where their "yes" would lead, yet they opened themselves up to God and put their lives in God's service. In our day, the challenge is the same, but the response differs. God, in the person of Christ Jesus, wants to be born again in our hearts and in our world. God awaits our "yes." We are far more cautious than either Joseph or Mary because we are not as willing to give our future over to God.

If this is to be the year that Christ will be born in our hearts, in our lives, in our world, we will have to change. Life will get messy, our values will shift, different things will have to become important to us. Well-intentioned friends and family will wonder where our old selves went and how they can get us back to normal. But once we say "yes" to God, our lives are forever changed.

**Prayer:**

*Lord, I hear your call and say "yes." Guide me, please.*

**Meditation:**

Do I have enough faith to find God in the messiness of my life?

# Monday of the Fourth Week

*O Radiant Dawn, splendor of eternal light, sun of justice: come, shine on those who dwell in darkness and the shadow of death.*
—EVENING PRAYER FROM THE LITURGY OF THE HOURS

The "O" antiphon for yesterday was suppressed because of the Fourth Sunday of Advent; but both yesterday's and today's antiphons deal with dwelling in darkness and in the shadow of death. We all have darkness in our lives and we all must learn how to dwell peacefully in the shadow of death, so it is important that these two themes are repeated.

In order to understand why the same image is being used two days in a row, recall the last time you had a conversation with someone who just would not listen. What do we do when someone will not listen to us? We repeat. We find different ways to say the same thing. We make our point over and over again until we are heard.

God keeps bringing up darkness and the shadow of death; we keep avoiding the issue, missing the point of such colorful language. God is the radiant dawn, the splendor of eternal light, the sun of justice. God is love but God is light, as well. God is the light that makes our faults most visible.

Several years ago, I hired a painter to do some work around the rectory. Since the rectory is very busy and crowded during the day, the painter worked at night. I remember being surprised when he brought in powerful lights to illumine the rooms that were being painted. When I asked why, his answer was clear and to the point: "I may have to paint at night, but my critics will examine by daylight." Would that we could learn to live our lives by that same philosophy. We may hide our less than virtuous deeds, we may take full advantage of the shadows of dusk to mute our selfish actions; but God will examine our lives in the bright light of his son. When Jesus is born, his presence will cast out all darkness; he will shine upon us and drive away the imperfections in our lives.

## Prayer:

*Lord, the time is near when I will celebrate your birth with all Christians. Let me honor your name in word and deed.*

## Meditation:

What darkness prevents me from seeing my sisters and brothers more clearly?

# Tuesday of the Fourth Week

*O King of all the nations, the only joy of every human heart;*
*O Keystone of the mighty arch of man, come and save*
*the creature you fashioned from the dust.*
—EVENING PRAYER FROM THE LITURGY OF THE HOURS

In today's "O" antiphon, God is recognized as the only joy of every heart. To be happy and joyful is strong motivation for human beings. It seems as if we are always in search of the one thing that is finally going to make us happy. Each day, each phase of our life seems to be consumed with the search for that one thing which is so elusive.

We work hard so we can make a lot of money. With the money we earn we buy things to make us happy. If we are smart, we soon realize that happiness cannot be purchased; if we are less smart, we may go on for years chasing the joy which money and material possessions forever promise but are incapable of delivering. I know too many people who feel cheated because they have bought all the right stuff—gadgets, toys, automobiles, homes, articles of clothing, and exclusive club memberships—yet finally have to admit that they were a lot happier when they lived in a second floor apartment and could still laugh at life.

The coming feast of Christmas shows just how devastating it can be to think that anything—or anyone, for that matter—is going to bring us joy. We will spend more money than has ever been spent in history lavishing gifts on one another, hoping that this will make us happy. We will open our hearts to receive our Savior but only the Savior who remains a child, stays in the manger where he belongs, and makes no demands on us or on our way of living.

Only the God who created us, fashioned us from dust, and put a seal on our hearts can bring us joy. St. Augustine was right when he said, "Our hearts are restless until they rest in you, O Lord!"

## Prayer:

*Lord, the birth of a child brings joy into our lives. As we prepare to celebrate Jesus' birth at Christmas, let me remember that true joy is found only in you.*

## Meditation:

What are the false gods that I believe will bring me joy?

# Wednesday of the Fourth Week

*O king and lawgiver, desire of the nations, Savior of all people,*
*come and set us free, Lord our God.*
—EVENING PRAYER FROM THE LITURGY OF THE HOURS

Emmanuel is the name given to Jesus by the angel, a name that means "God is with us." How does that name apply to us here and now? Perhaps we can consider all the millions of people who have been born; think of the relatively minute number of people whom we will have met in our lifetime, out of the all the people who have walked on the earth. Think of how, out of infinite possibilities, God gave us our own special parents who helped us grow into the people we are. Think of the teachers who saw the goodness in us and did not stop at the obstacles we put in their way. Stop and count the friends who have entered and left our lives, or have never left. Consider all the fortunate occurrences that have fashioned us. In short, when we see how God has gently yet forcefully guided the events and people that have made up our lives, we know God is Emmanuel—we know God is with us!

This divine serendipity, this fortuitous shaping of our lives, does not mean that things always run smoothly, or that our parents are perfect, or that our friends and teachers are right on target all the time. It does not mean there are no other jobs we could do, no other way to make our mark in the world other than the one we have chosen. It does mean that out of the plethora of possibilities, God selects wisely. We should be thankful for all the ways God has been present to us, the ways that God has been Emmanuel.

With a lover's heart we prepare to celebrate Jesus' birth not just as an historical event but as present and future event, as well. God is born in our lives over and over again. Christmas is the day to thank God for being born into our world, into our hearts. With the whole church we pray that God will once again set us free: free to embrace the gift of life along with its possibilities; free to be God's people and to build up the kingdom.

## Prayer:

*I have prepared a path for you. Come, Lord Jesus!*

## Meditation:

Where is God being born in my life today?

# Christmas Eve

*Blessed be the Lord the God of Israel because he has visited and ransomed his people.* LK 1:67–79

When I was a teenager, my mother invited two of the priests from the local seminary to dinner one night. This event was a very big deal. The house was cleaner than ever. We ate in the dining room instead of the kitchen. The table was covered with Irish linen, and the special china, usually reserved for Thanksgiving, Christmas, and Easter, was carefully set out. Looking out the door, impatiently waiting for the arrival of the priests, we were given last-minute orders on how to behave. Then the guests arrived.

We all sat in the living room and went through the usual preliminary pleasantries of a visit. Finally, we gathered at the table and one of the priests said grace. My oldest brother, Jerry, took care of breaking the ice. He picked up the freshly-ironed Irish linen napkin from under his fork, held it up like a foreign object, and in a very clear voice asked my mother if it was okay to use the good napkins. A momentary hush fell over the room. My mother gave my brother "the look" and tension began mounting, when one of the priests said, "I was just wondering the same thing myself." Nervous laughter slowly gave way to good-natured laughter and the visit became a time that everyone could enjoy.

Tomorrow God will visit us. We will "put on the dog" for a while. Eventually we will realize that our God comes as One like us, though free from sin. In a burst of divine love, God took on our human condition so that from within and among us God might teach us how to live and what to value. In ancient times it was said that God pitched a tent among us. Today we can say that God rings the doorbell, calls on the phone, or leaves a message on our e-mail. May we open our hearts to a visit from God and welcome God to the innermost places of our lives.

## Prayer:

*Lord, may I greet you as I am, and answer the invitation to become one of your holy people, a true child of God.*

## Meditation:

Do I dare to meet God in the ordinary events of my life?

# Christmas Day

*Mary treasured all these things and reflected on them in her heart.*
*The shepherds returned, glorifying and praising God for all they*
*had heard and seen, in accord with what had been told them.*
LK 2:15–20

Today we are given the most precious gift of all: a child. We have been waiting for this day. Now it has arrived, and we are confronted with the mystery of life.

Like Mary, we need to learn how to treasure this gift. Like Mary, we need to reflect on the gift of Jesus in our hearts. Mary shows us the way. Like any first-time parent, she holds and caresses her child as he cries out in need, making demands. Mary will come to know that this child will profoundly change what we know as life.

Like Mary and Joseph, we need to look on an infant and see the future. We need to remember that a child is permission from God to dream, to believe in a future that will make the present dull by comparison. There is a wonderful expression: "A child is proof that God has not yet given up on us." Jesus is our proof that God will never give up on us.

Sometime today, in the midst of all the excitement, all the gift giving and receiving, family meals, and visits to special people, let us find some quiet time and be still with the child Jesus. Let us look deeply into the eyes of hopefulness, examine the hands that will one day heal, caress the feet that will propel this child on the journey called life. Today's Gospel acclamation says all that needs to be said: "Alleluia! Good News and great joy to all the world! Today is born our Savior, Christ the Lord. Alleluia!"

## Prayer:

*Alleluia! Today is born our Savior, Christ, the Lord!*

## Meditation:

How will the gift of hope and new life brought by the birth of the Christ Child affect my life and my heart this year?